CHURCHMAN'S CIGARETTES

J. C. CLAY

J. SULLIVAN (WIGAN)

WILLS'S CIGARETTES.

H. M. BOWCOTT.

A. H. DYSON.

PLAYER'S CIGARETTES.

IDRIS RICHARDS

OGDEN'S CIG...

J. BLAIR,
CARDIFF CITY.

F. KEENOR

...RERAS CIGARETTES

E. BLENKINSOP

LIVERPOOL (1ST DIVISION)

PLAYER'S CIGARETTES.

W. J. DELAHAY

G. NICHOLSON
CARDIFF CITY

WILLS'S CIGARETTES

JOHN
ROBERTS

OGDEN'S CIGARETTES.

JIM DRISCOLL.

CARDIFF
Yesterday

End papers:

Cigarette cards reached the zenith of their popularity in the inter-war years. One of the most popular subjects was sport and to be included in a series guaranteed a measure of immortality. The sportsmen featured gave outstanding entertainment to Cardiffians and with the exception of Wilf Wooller the cards are captioned. For the record here are the names of the issuing companies:

J. C. Clay, A. H. Dyson and C. Smart—W. A. & A. C. Churchman's 'Cricketers, 1936';

M. J. Turnbull—Ardath's 'Cricket, Tennis and Golf Personalities, 1935';

Dai Davies—John Player's 'Cricketers, 1930';

J. Mercer—W. D. & H. O. Wills' 'Cricketers, 1928';

T. Arnott—W. D. & H. O. Wills' 'Cricketers, 1929';

Jack Peterson—Godfrey Phillips, 1937; Jim Driscoll—Ogden's 'Pugilists and Wrestlers', 1908;

Wilf Wooller—R. & J. Hill's 'Celebrities of Sport', 1939;

H. M. Bowcott, Frank Williams and John Roberts—

W. D. & H. O. Wills' 'Rugby Internationals', caricatured by Mel, 1929;

A. Skym—W. A. & A. C. Churchman's 'Rugby Internationals, 1935'; Len Davies, Idris Richards

and W. J. Delahay—John Player's 'Footballers', caricatured by Rip, 1926;

J. Sullivan—Ogden's 'Football Club Captains, 1936';

A. Turner (Cardiff City), in Doncaster Rovers strip—Carreras' 'Popular Footballers, 1934';

T. Watson—John Player's 'Football Caricatures by Mac', 1927;

J. Blair—Ogden's 'Captains of Association Football Clubs and Colours', 1926;

E. Blenkinsop (later with Cardiff City)—Carreras' 'Footballers, 1934';

G. Nicholson—R. & J. Hill's 'Famous Footballers, 1939';

Fred Keenor (card issued when he had joined Tunbridge Wells Rangers as player-manager

in 1935-36)—Godfrey Phillips' 'International Caps', 1936.

1 The southern end of St Mary Street decorated for the visit of the Prince and Princess of Wales (later King Edward VII and Queen Alexandra) with their daughters the Princesses Maud and Victoria on 27 June 1896. They visited the great Cathays Park Exhibition and opened the completed Central Library

STEWART WILLIAMS'

CARDIFF

Yesterday

Book Eight

Foreword by
Roy Denning

First Published April, 1984

© Stewart Williams, Publishers,
1 Trem-y-Don, Barry,
South Glamorgan

ISBN 0 900807 61 X

ACKNOWLEDGEMENTS

We extend our grateful thanks to the following for giving us permission to use their photographs:-

Dave Ames (100, 168); John F. Andrews (76); Victor Antippas (40, 41, 63, 64); Bill Barrett (78, 90); Bob Bradley (125); Christopher Brain (157); Mr & Mrs A. R. Brind (42, 92, 95, 96, 164, 165); Cliff Brown (74, 75, 199); Cardiff Central Library (1, 2, 5, 6, 7, 38); Eric H. Chamberlain (56, 184, 185, 187, 188, 189); Dennis Charles (108, 210); Gordon E. Cirel (136); Jack Cross (46, 204); J. E. Crowley (207, 209); James A. Davey (54, 55); Tommy Davies (134); Roy Denning (126); R. G. Dite (171); Mrs G. M. Donovan (128); Mrs C. Edwards (192); Mrs Georgina Empsall (148); Lionel V. Evans (212, 213, 214); Mrs Valerie Farmar (48, 105, 106); H. Forster (175); Miss Reta Gale (127, 190); T. Gardiner (68, 69); Ken Good (149); Fred Goodall (121, 122); K. F. Goslin (61, 62); Roy Griffin (203); Mrs Lucy Haines (162, 174); Mrs Jennifer Hampton (36, 37, 59); D. F. Hampson (70, 71); G. Hanlan (103, 114); Mrs D. Herbert (107, 109, 169, 196); Noel F. Ingram (113, 130, 131, 132, 133, 208); Mrs F. James (201); Mrs Pauline James (202); F. N. Jenkins (30, 51, 57, 58); Fred Jones (3, 4, 9, 10, 11, 12, 13, 14, 15, 16, 17, 18, 20, 32, 33, 35, 43, 44, 45, 47, 49, 60, 66, 67, 84, 85, 98, 117, 120, 145, 186, 191, 193, 195, 197, 200); Mrs F. Leach (194); Miss R. M. Legg (8, 34, 50, 72, 73, 83); Tommy Letton (173); Mrs John Lloyd (167); Mrs Diana Lomax (36, 37, 59); Mr & Mrs T. R. Lusty (19, 31); A. Maidment (53); Simon Mansfield (87, 144); E. & N. Matthews (94, 211); James P. McIntyre (112); S. C. Mead (129); Con Mullett (170); Mrs Marjorie Neil (166); C. Nicholls (161); G. H. Nowell (172); T. O'Keefe (163); E. Oram (160); Arthur J. Porter (86, 99, 111, 116, 206); Geoffrey Pritchard (21, 22, 23, 24, 25, 28, 52, 79, 80, 81, 82, 118, 119, 123, 124, 156); Ken Pudge (176, 177, 178, 179); Mrs S. E. Reed-Smith (89); Billy Rees (150, 151); J. A. Simmonds (91, 104); Mrs C. Simon (39); Mrs Ivy Sparkes (88, 101, 102, 110); Martin Stephens (93); Chris Taylor (135, 137, 146, 147); Jim Union (77, 198, 205); Haydn Vaughan (97, 159); L. G. Watkins (138); Gordon Westcott (152, 153, 155, 158); W. 'Knocker' White (115, 154); Cress Wiggin (182, 183); Mac Williams (180, 181); John Worrell (139, 140, 141, 142, 143).

Printed in Wales by D. Brown & Sons Ltd., Cowbridge and Bridgend, Glamorgan

Foreword

by Roy Denning

'You can always tell a man from Mars', remarked the little old lady in the black straw hat, 'by the fact that he walks six inches from the ground.' I was not too impressed by this gem of little-known information because, apart from the fey gleam in her eye, she was also convinced that the leader of the latest band of UFO-borne visitors to our planet had taken to peering at her through the window above her front door. Such brushes with fantasy enlivened for me the sometimes humdrum existence of a library assistant in Cardiff Central Library.

The interplanetary peeping Toms had a less whimsical counterpart in the dreams of T. C. Jones, a sombrely-dressed old man who plodded into the reference library every day, taking always the same seat before opening a battered attache case and spreading on the table a number of press cuttings. The yellowing bits of paper represented the summit of his life's achievement, the departure point for his personal fantasy of what might have been, for T. C. Jones had once stood for Parliament and been narrowly beaten.

The T. C. Joneses of this world usually evoke sympathy, even from library staff, accustomed as they are to public displays of the vagaries of human nature, but there were those among the readers for whom unqualified sympathy was an inappropriate response. There was one female reader, who shall remain nameless, whose clothes and whole person reeked of fish. She could scatter the Saturday morning queue at the lending library counter like autumn leaves, a facility shared by Charlie, an elegantly-dressed meths drinker with a purple countenance. But it is Cliff, the down-and-out student of the *Financial Times*, who remains most vividly in my memory. Always attired in the same ragged jacket, shirt open to the waist from lack of buttons, with a cigarette-end hanging from his lower lip as if glued to that unlovely feature, he was barely tolerated by staff and porters alike. When I refused his request for a Christmas present, he remarked with withering scorn that he could 'buy and sell' me, so it was not surprising that, after his death from pneumonia in his dingy room, he was found to have over six thousand pounds in his possession.

The lighter side of library life was sometimes overshadowed by the dark, inescapable clouds of reality. One of my duties as a very junior assistant in the lending library was to set out armfuls of fiction in the shelves reserved for newly-returned novels. It was wartime and the turnover in romantic authors such as Ethel M. Dell and Dornford Yates was brisk. It was a routine which demanded the nimbleness of youth, for one needed a turn of speed and a dazzling sidestep to avoid being trampled underfoot in the rush for the literary delicacies. The charge was normally led by two young sisters, whose presence was necessary for the proper conduct of the ritual, but one day they were missing from their post and they were never again to lead the assault. The previous night there had been an air raid, in which a stick of bombs had been dropped across the town centre, straddling the library. One actually fell in the light well in the middle of the building, while another hit a house in Frederick Street. The two girls had taken shelter in this house, which was not their home, and had been killed. This tragic incident had its own grim humour however, for the library bomb destroyed the toilets and for some considerable time the staff were to be seen wending their way to the public toilets at the Hayes Island, clutching special passes.

From the lending library I was eventually transferred to the reference library, where I worked with personalities well-known and respected in their time, but too numerous to deal with adequately here. One character must not be allowed to slide into oblivion, however, namely A. E. ('Tubby') Sleight, reference librarian and true-blue Yorkshireman. 'Tubby' had served in the 1914-18 war in the Royal Artillery, but his lack of inches confined him to the role of mule-driver, but even here he had difficulties, for he could not see properly over the mules' ears. Riding off the parade ground was a special problem for 'Tubby', for he could not reach the stirrup and was reduced to scrambling up the mule's front leg.

Of all the associations formed during more than seventeen years at the Central Library none was to prove more lasting and fruitful than a chance meeting with Stewart Williams, publisher extraordinary. I have had the privilege of assisting in the production of many of his publications, but *Cardiff Yesterday* is Stewart's own brainchild. For this unique series he has succeeded in enlisting the support of librarians, archivists, local historians, postcard collectors and general public, in a communal effort to preserve for future generations our visual memories. No fantasy here, or high-stepping men from Mars, but places and things as they were and real faces from the past. Long may the series continue.

AUTHOR'S NOTE

It falls to very few people to make a livelihood from doing what they enjoy most, so I consider myself fortunate to be in the publishing game and not only surviving but making new friends with each succeeding volume of *Cardiff Yesterday*. The series has been outstandingly successful and goes from strength to strength as Cardiffians from all walks of life and points of the compass join together on a nostalgic journey down the years. I have lost count of the number of family reunions we have accidentally brought about. Letters always follow publication and this surely is what the series is all about, the immensely satisfying business of rekindling old memories, reviving happy moments from the past, and putting on visual record for posterity what evidence still exists of the Cardiff many of us remember before sweeping changes carried it out of sight and mind.

My thanks are again due to the 'inner cabinet' who contribute so much to the finished article: Geoff Dart, former County Librarian of South Glamorgan, whose incomparable knowledge of the city's history and painstaking research guarantee a high standard of annotation; Bill Barrett, another local historian of repute and an authority on baseball; and Fred Jones, whose magnificent collection of post-cards has added considerably to the quality of the series. I depend on an enthusiastic band of 'scouts' to keep the pictures flowing and in the forefront are old friends Bill and Dennis O'Neill. Another good friend is Chris Taylor, whose knowledge of transport continually surprises me and who can always be relied upon to help out. As can be seen from the acknowledgements, 73 different donors have supplied pictures. Perhaps I can add a special word of thanks to Cardiff Central Library, Mr & Mrs A. R. Brind, Eric H. Chamberlain, Noel F. Ingram and Geoffrey Pritchard for their exceptional kindnesses, also to my son Robert Williams whose camera skills I have been pleased to draw upon in this volume. You will have noticed the colourful cigarette card reproductions of Cardiff sportsmen featured in our end-papers. They belong to collector Gordon Westcott of Machen, a prominent member of South Glamorgan Cartophilic Society, to whom I am deeply grateful both for the idea and the use of his valuable originals.

Publicity is always welcome but it should be deserved and for making sure my feet stay on the ground I wish to thank my old friend Geoff Rich, editor of the *South Wales Echo*, whose direct but kindly advice has helped me to shape the series. Another friend, Frank Hennessy, has always shown a keen personal interest and given valuable air-time on his CBC programme.

My final word of thanks goes to Roy Denning who wrote the foreword. We share many interests and come from the same Ely background, so it is a special pleasure to publish his amusing recollections of life as a young library assistant in Cardiff Central Library.

1 Trem-y-Don,
Barry, CF6 8QJ

STEWART WILLIAMS

City, Suburbs and Docks

2 The junction of Duke Street, High Street and Castle Street as it looked in 1921. Two years later the buildings on the left (north side) of Duke Street were demolished to remove a bottleneck which had caused serious traffic congestion for many years

The Hayes, Cardiff.

M. J. R. ... B. No 6072

3 The David Morgan building dominates The Hayes in this 1910 view

4 East end of Queen Street in 1904 before the construction of the Capitol. Three of these shops were built on the front garden of a former large residence, Spring Gardens House. Here in 1838-42 lived Capt. (later Admiral) W. H. Smyth, his wife and daughter Henrietta who were the grandparents and mother of the future Lord Baden-Powell

Queen St., Cardiff.   No. 685.

5/6 Two views of Queen Street in the early 1900s. (*Above*) David Evans was one of the first tenants of Andrews Buildings in 1896. Founded by Solomon and Emile Andrews in conjunction with David Evans the company continued in business until 1919 when the Evans family was bought out and the name changed to Asher Hart Ltd.
(*Below*) the *Park Hotel* dominates this view

7 A bird's eye view of Cardiff from the Castle clock tower looking south, *c.*1908. The corner of Castle Street and Womanby Street is just out of camera (*bottom left*). The roof of the *Globe* can be seen and also (*middle left*) the glass roof of both arms of the Castle Arcade

8 Pre-First World War view from Clare Road looking south to Paget Street and to the western end of Penarth Road. The Anastasia Greek Restaurant now occupies the site of E. D. Evans' post office, stationery and ironmongery shop

9 Salisbury Road in 1908 looked much as it does today except for the tram lines. The Cathays route has seen horse trams, electric trams and was the first to be converted to low-bridge double decker motor buses in January 1930

10/11 The northern residential suburb of Rhiwbina has managed to develop while at the same time retaining its 'garden village' flavour. (*Above*) Taken in 1928 showing the 'bus terminus at that time at the junction of Heol-y-Deri and Beulah Road; (*below*) practically the same view in 1963

12   Newport Road, Rumney, in 1932

13   Church Road, Whitchurch, in 1910

14 The commencement of Penylan Road from Blenheim Road going north-west to its junction
with Wellfield Road and Ninian Road as it looked in 1908. In October 1902 the Public Works
Committee resolved that this portion of Penylan Road be renamed Pant-yr-Wyn Crescent, but the
Borough Council 'eliminated' the minute on a petition of 25 owner-occupiers

15 Albany Road in 1908. The bungalow shop and adjoining private residence were demolished in
1913-14 to make way for the Penylan (later Globe) Cinema

16   Kincraig Street from City Road, 1906. In the background is the former Plasnewydd Mansion the ancestral home of the Richards family and from 1890 the Mackintosh Institute

17   Keppoch Street, Roath, in 1910. About 1928 Davies's Commercial College was established in the large corner house on the extreme left and is still in existence under changed ownership

Romilly Crescent, Cardiff.

18 Romilly Crescent, Canton, in 1906 with in the distance Solomon Andrews's horse 'buses
about to pass on their journeys between High Street, Llandaff, and Castle Street

19 Kingsland Road, Canton, in the early years of this century

Feeding the Seal in Victoria Park, Canton Cardiff

20 'Billy the seal' was really a female grey seal. She came to Victoria Park in 1912 and remained there, apart from brief escapes when the River Ely overflowed, until her death in 1939. Immortalised by Frank Hennessy, she is part of Cardiff folk-lore

21 The *Cow & Snuffers* is on the far right in this 1930 view of the Glamorganshire Canal and Lock at Llandaff North

Canal & Lock Llandaff North

22 High Street, Llandaff, in the 1920s

23 Half way along the north-east side of The Green is the City Cross which, according to tradition, is the place where Archbishop Baldwin preached the Third Crusade on his journey through Wales in 1188. The cross was restored and reset in 1897. This was taken before the First World War

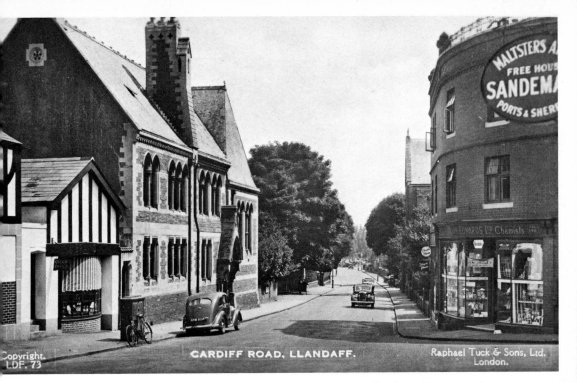

CARDIFF ROAD, LLANDAFF.

24 Cardiff Road, Llandaff, taken in 1938. The Probate Registry (*left*), where wills are recorded and verified, was designed by John Pritchard and built in 1857. It is considered a splendid example of Victorian design

25 River bridge, Llandaff North, *c.*1925. Hailey Park, given to the city in 1924, appears to be fenced in and paths laid. This was done before the official opening by the Lord Mayor on 3 May 1926

River Bridge, Llandaff North. 896.

26 Fairwater brook gives geographical meaning to this delightful rural view taken in the early 1930s. The thatched house has long since gone and been replaced by the *Fairwater Hotel*

27 Thatched cottages nestling into the hillside add to the timeless charm of St Fagans village. This was taken before the Second World War

28 The brook is the only readily identifiable feature in this 1920s view of Fairwater taken before housing development transformed this once rural district of Cardiff

29 This fountain in Llandaff Fields was erected in 1900 at the expense of Mrs H. M. Thompson of nearby 'Whitley Batch', the Council providing the water supply. The stonework is still in situ but the water has been cut off for many years

30 The weir on the River Ely at Leckwith in 1941 prior to the improvement scheme which changed its course

31 The business heart of Cardiff's dockland in 1908

32/33   The John Cory Sailors' and Soldiers' Rest at 179-180 Bute Street as it looked in 1905. It was equally impressive from the outside and inside. Indeed the floral hall seems to have had an almost palm court atmosphere. Erected in 1901-02 it replaced an earlier sailors' rest at 180 and a lodging house at 179

34 The year is 1914 and even as the sun shines in Bute Street the storm clouds of war are gathering. Soon life will be changed dramatically for most of the men in the picture

35 The spoils of war proudly on display as a propaganda exercise during the First World War

3 German Boats handed over to Allies in Cardiff Dock. 993.

36/37 Frank Jones (*second left*), a Cardiff pharmacist, probably originated the idea of fumigating ships' holds using cyanide gas. It proved most effective in controlling the vermin, as can be seen from these photographs taken in 1930. Older readers may remember Frank Jones's pharmacy on the corner of the Castle Arcade in Castle Street (see No.59)

38 A 1923 aerial view of Cardiff Docks looking north with the Bute East Dock (*centre*) and the Roath Dock just visible at the foot of the photograph

Trade and Industry

39 The impressive facade of Noah Rees & Sons' premises in Working Street in 1900. Through the entrance and behind the building was one of Cardiff's residential courts, Thomas's Terrace, used by Noah Rees for storage etc. It disappeared with the left-hand three quarters of the building *c.*1963 for the Fine Fare (now Primark) building; the remaining right-hand quarter is now the only unit on the east side of Working Street surviving from pre-1960. The remains of the lettering 'Warehouses' can still be deciphered

40 William Fry's pork butchers' shop in Bridge Street titillated many Edwardian taste buds with this window display

41   By the 1920s William Fry had also established himself in the Central Market

42   R. J. Brind's bread and confectionery shop in Cowbridge Road, Canton, c.1923. Welsh cakes were 4 for one penny, scones and doughnuts a half-penny each, and a large white loaf 3½d. The shop was first opened in 1913 and transferred to Fairwater in 1937

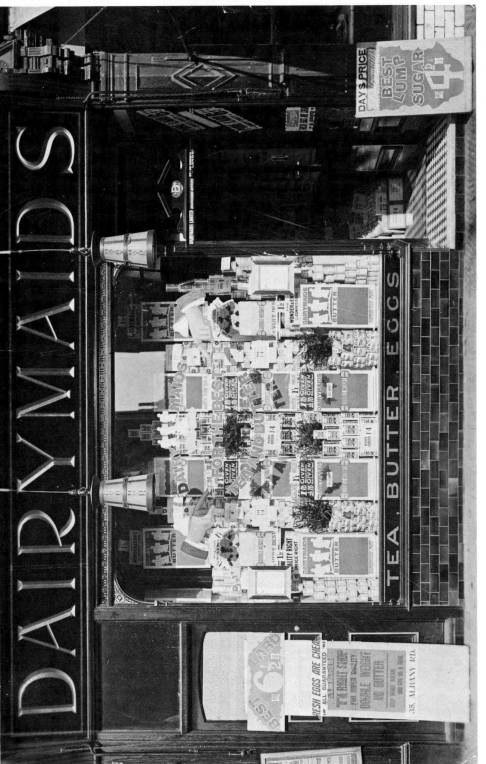

43 Dairymaids, 35 Albany Road, one of four shops (the others were in Crwys Road, Cowbridge Road and Penarth) which were in business for a short time from 1914 to some time in 1916. No doubt the onset of food shortages and rationing in the later years of the First World War affected their trade

44 H. J. Prosser's steam bakery was situated in Bruce Street, Cathays. This was taken outside
Roath Park in 1927

45 Cardiff Dairy Company ran a successful business from 47 Atlas Road, Canton. Charles
Banwell was the proprietor when this was taken in 1927

46 Half a century before MacFisheries occupied the site a Mr Gray ran a fish and poultry business at 106 Queen Street. He is the man in the boater. Holding the horse's head is Ernie Cross, father of the donor. Taken 1907-08

47 Frayling's carried on business in City Road for over 30 years after this was taken in 1901. The house partly visible on the left was demolished along with its neighbour to make way for the Gaiety Electric Theatre in 1912

48 Lamerton & Son's butchers' shop at 236 City Road, *c*.1924. The young assistant on the right is the late John Farmar who subsequently became well-known in the motor trade in Cardiff

49 Heath Stores (J. & M. Redwood), Birchgrove, in 1932. This and the adjoining premises were demolished in 1967 for a redevelopment scheme. The original address was 51 Philog Road

50/51 William Hancock founded his brewery in Crawshay Street, Cardiff, in 1884 and quickly built a reputation for fine ales. With the introduction of mechanical transport, deliveries to the city, suburbs and surrounding areas was made easier. Among the earliest vehicles were these *c*.1920 solid-tyre lorries; (*below*) the fleet had expanded sufficiently by 1930 to employ this fine body of men solely on transport duties

Progress Series Printed in England.   T. H. & S. Co. B. & C.
"THE COW & SNUFFERS." LLANDAFF NORTH, GLAM. NO. 320.
Visited by Disraeli when paying his addresses to his future wife at Green Meadow.

52 The *Cow & Snuffers,* Llandaff North, *c.*1900. It was partly demolished in 1905 to make way for the present building. Doubt has always surrounded Disraeli's visit. He himself denied it although his secretary Lord Rowton said his master spent a night there having been intrigued by the name

53 The *Locomotive Inn* on the corner of Broadway and Nora Street, 1912. Nora Street has since been renamed Helen Place and the pub is now *The Locomotive*

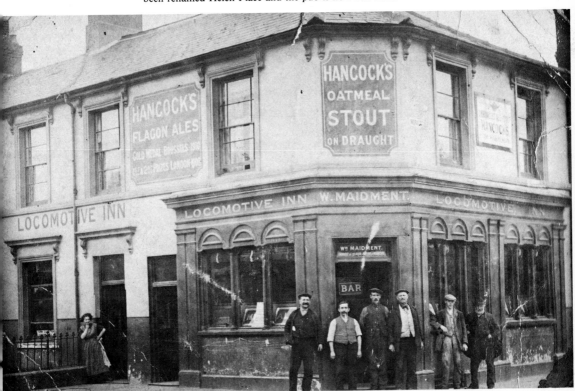

54/55 Many readers will remember Sam Davey who kept the *Roath Park Hotel* in City Road from the late 20s until his death in 1940. A Belfast man, he married a daughter (Mabel) of William Davies who ran the *Mount Stuart Hotel*

56 Ind Coope brewers' dray outside the *Wyndham Hotel*, Canton, *c.*1923. The donor, Eric H. Chamberlain, was born there and his father, Harold P. Chamberlain, managed it. The family ran numerous Cardiff pubs from 1881 until they ceased trading in 1977 including the *Victoria*, Queen Street, *Terminus*, St Mary Street, and *Bertram*, Roath

57/58 Mr and Mrs S. C. Jenkins and family pose outside the *Rose & Crown* in Millicent Street shortly before its demolition in August 1936. The pub was owned by William Hancock and Mr Jenkins was the last licensee

A previous licensee was 'Peerless Jim' Driscoll's brother-in-law James Donovan who kept the *Rose & Crown* from 1918 until his death in 1929 aged 60. His first wife née Mary Ann Driscoll died in 1922 aged 45

59 Frank Jones's pharmacy on the corner of the Castle Arcade in Castle Street, *c.*1930 (see Nos. 36/37)

60 Carpenters and joiners, brickies and stonemasons, plumbers and even foremen posed for posterity outside their St Mary Street depot in July 1916

61/62 The old established firm of tea merchants, Phillips & Co, were at 74 Queen Street from the 1880s until 1913 when they moved to Edward Terrace. (*Above*) Staff outing to the Gower Coast in 1929; (*below*) taken in the 1930s. Note the tree-lined Dock Feeder in the background

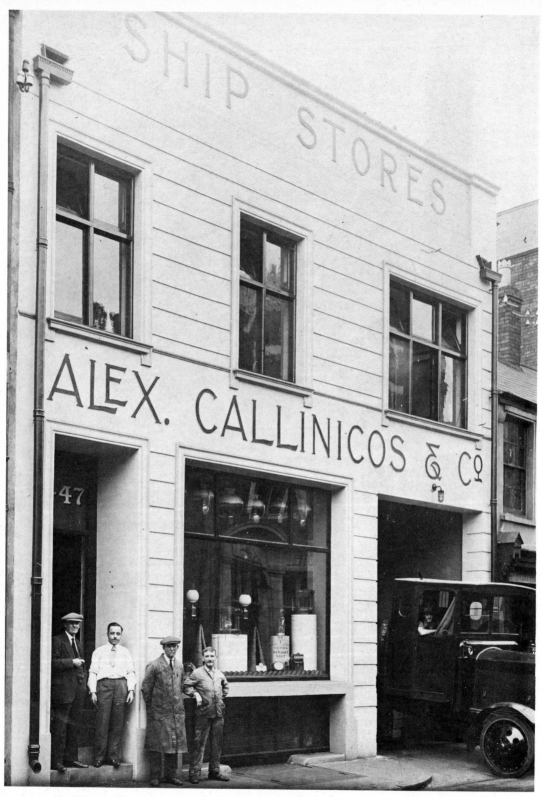

63 Ship chandler Alex Callinicos traded for 75 years from premises in George Street. The donor's father, Alexander Antippas, is standing second left in shirt sleeves

64 John Williams, chief storeman at Callinicos, at work shortly befor the business was closed down in 1980

65 Staff employed by Joseph Lucas Ltd, Penarth Road, taken about 1940

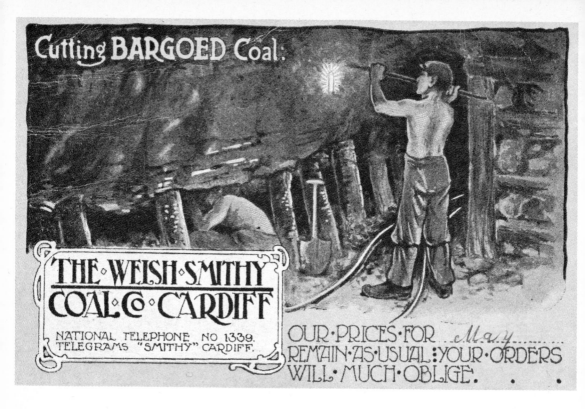

66/67   Trade cards used by the Welsh Smithy Coal Company of 51 George Street, Docks. Both were posted in 1905. The company was in business at the same address for over 40 years

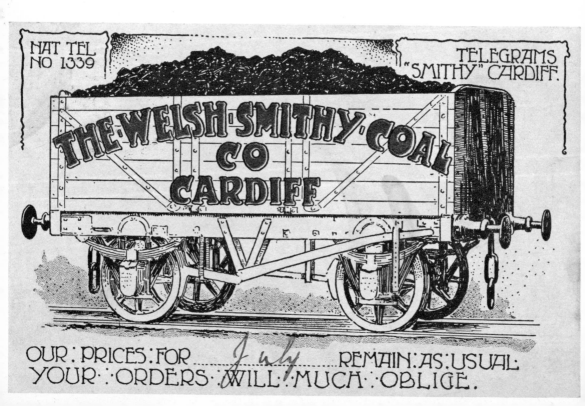

68/69 The coachbuilding firm of William Lewis & Sons (Cardiff) Ltd, was founded in 1886 and produced many thousands of bodies—horse-drawn in the old days and later private and commercial motor vehicles—from their Tudor Lane workshops. (*Above*) Part of the work-force taken *c.*1930; (*below*) staff on an annual outing to the West Country in July, 1939. The firm continued in business until the 1970s

70/71 Bell & Nicolson Ltd, the Midlands-based textile wholesalers, occupied these premises in North Edward Street at the rear of the Capitol for many years before closing down their Cardiff operations in July 1981. (*Above*) As the premises appeared in 1924, and (*below*) in 1927 after extension

72/73 Employees of Robinson David & Company Ltd, timber merchants and importers, at the firm's Herbert Street sawmills in 1909; (*below*) Robinson David staff-outing about to depart from the Civic Centre in 1930

74/75 Employees of the Phoenix Brickworks, Birchgrove, at work and play. (*Above*) In the yard at Caerphilly Road; (*below*) all ready for the annual outing. Both were taken in 1930

76 A number of well-known Cardiff businessmen are in this group taken on a visit by the East
Wales Division of the Institute of the Motor Trade to the Wandsworth Works of Vacuum Oil Co.
Ltd, on 20 June 1933

77 White Wilson's (Kosirest) furniture and bedding factory situated in York Place, Grangetown,
near the Gasworks and on the site of the the old horse-drawn tram depot. During the Second
World War production switched to making ammunition boxes

Religion, Education and Public Service

78 *(opposite)* Religion in Cardiff was taken far more seriously a hundred years ago than it is today. The church seen here *c.*1900 (and still standing) is St Stephen's in Mount Stuart Square. It was established as a result of a split between the old St Mary the Virgin congregation and was known as the 'tin church' because the nave was originally constructed from corrugated iron sheets. Nowadays the old troubles are forgotten and the two parishes are once again united, St Stephen's now ministering from the converted parish hall in Evelyn Street with Father Jordan looking after the united parish

79 Archdeacon James Rice Buckley who gave 46 years of devoted ministry to the diocese of Llandaff

80 Archdeacon Buckley's statue by Goscombe John on Llandaff Green was unveiled on 30 October 1926

A·MAN·HE·WAS
TO·ALL
THE·COUNTRY·DEAR

JAMES·RICE·BUCKLEY
1878·VICAR·OF·LLANDAFF·1924
ARCHDEACON·OF·LLANDAFF
1913 — 1924

LLANDAFF. ARCHDEACON BUCKLEY MEMORIAL.   63790.

81 All Saints Sunday School class, Llandaff North, *c*.1900. Edward David of Eagle Foundry, Llandaff North, is in the centre

82 All Saints, Llandaff North, young men's class, *c*.1900

83   St Barnabas church choir, *c.*1900

84   A group of distinguished onlookers outside Cardiff Castle on 12 July 1914 watching the crowds in the streets before the procession in the Castle Grounds during the National Catholic Congress

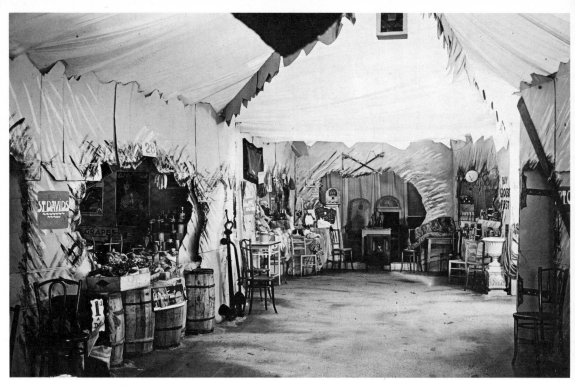

85 A fund-raising bazaar at St David's Church Hall, Ely, in the 1930s

86 Harvest Thanksgiving at Hannah Street Congregational Church, Docks, 1945

87 'The Gipsies', seen in Walker's Field, Corbett Road, were members of Wood Street Sisterhood

88 Salvation Army (Stuart Hall) band on the steps of the Law Courts in 1931

STUART HALL BAND, CARDIFF 1931.

89 A combined Cardiff schools visit to Porthcawl Camp in 1954

90 Portraits of sports stars Terry Yorath, Colin Baker, Billy Boston, Phil Edwards and Joe Erskine—all 'old boys' of Cardiff Central Youth Club—were drawn by members and exhibited as part of the club's 60th anniversary celebrations in 1979. Here Benny Farrugia is working on his drawing of Terry Yorath, watched by fascinated younger members

91   Form IVa, Canton High School, 1944-45

92   Canton High School, first year class 1954-55

93 Metal Street School, 1919

94 Party time at Adamsdown Infants' School, 1936

95 Severn Road Infants' School, 1921-22. The teacher was Miss Thomas

96 Severn Road Boys' School, 1922-23. The teacher was Mr Richards

97 Standard 3a, Severn Road Boys' School, 1923

98 Severn Road Infants' School, September 1925

99   Standard 1, Splotlands Elementary School, *c.*1923

100   Splotlands Infants' School, 1938

101   Wood Street School, 1924

102   Wood Street School, June 1927

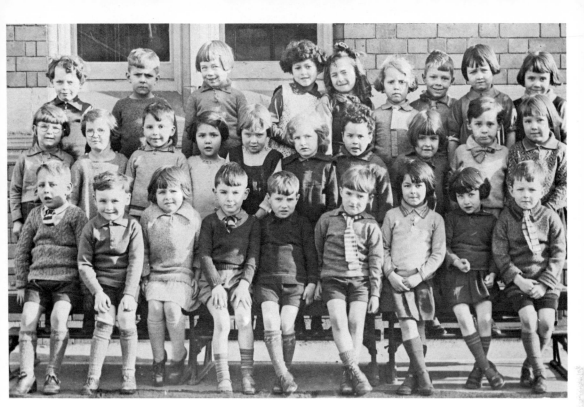

103 Marlborough Road School, *c.*1934

104 Herbert Thompson School, Ely, *c.*1934

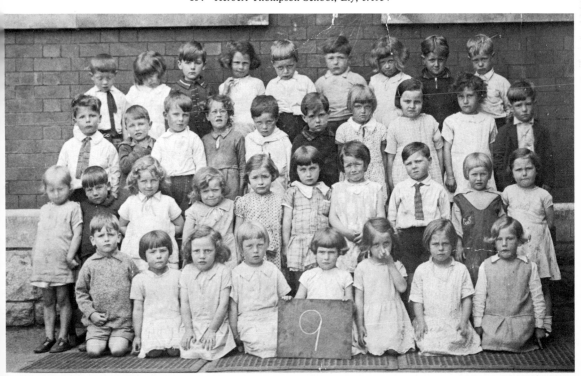

105/106 The principals and cast of an operetta performed by the staff and pupils of the old Rumney Council School *c.*1922 under the direction of their headmaster Mr Matthewson, a well-known local figure. The school stood close to Wentloog Road on part of the site now occupied by Rumney Junior School

107   Standard 1a, Court Road School, Grangetown, 1931

108   Ely Council School, *c.*1935

109 Standard 1, Marlborough Road School, 1931

110 Pupils of Wood Street School with their teacher, Miss Hardy, 1933

111 Form 2, Howard Gardens Municipal Secondary School, 1928. The teacher was Mr John

112 Form 1, St Illtyd's College, taken at the College playing fields at Blackweir *c*.1929

113 St Edward's Church Youth Club, Roath, when formed in 1945. Membership grew to over 100 under the leadership of Noel F. Ingram and patronage of Rev. T. Bevan

114 Coronation fancy dress at Marlborough Road School, 1953

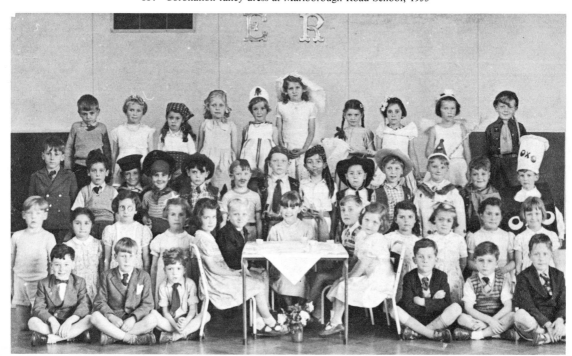

115 The Melingriffith Volunteer and Cadet Corps Sports Club in camp at Penzance in 1928

116 Training course for officers and NCO's of Cardiff Battalion, Boys' Brigade, at Jubilee Camp, Porthcawl, c.1942. Prominent BB stalwarts such as Reg Pye, Tom Coakley, Joe Ponsford, Alf Barratt, Bill Miller, Herbert Hambly and Tom Cox are included

117   St Stephen's Scouts parading in Mount Stuart Square, 1912

118   2nd Llandaff Scout Group, August 1937

119   Dennis fire engine at a display in Sophia Gardens in 1941. This vehicle was the last to be delivered in 'fire engine red' before the establishment of the National Fire Service and served the city until the early 1960s

120   Show of strength from the Police outside the American Roller Rink in Westgate Street where they were billeted during the 1911 strike

121/122 Members of the Auxiliary Fire Service outside their station at Hope Street, Cardiff Docks, in 1940. The Vauxhall car (*below*) was used by Prime Minister Winston Churchill when he visited the city

123/124 The Rt. Hon. Herbert Morrison, Home Secretary, visited Cardiff in 1942 and is here seen (*above*) inspecting NFS personnel outside the City Hall. (*Below*) NFS parade along Westgate Street during the Home Secretary's visit

125 ARP staff who operated in the Canton area during the Second World War. Among the wardens is Jack Evans, ex-Cardiff City star (*fifth from right, standing*)

126 Maindy Depot first aid party, winners of the Civil Defence Casualty Services Competition, December 1942. K. F. Bullen (holding cup) was captain

127 Patients and staff at St Mellons Convalescent Home in 1930

128 Land Army girls at Witla Court hostel, Rumney, 1945. They worked on Ford's farm at St Mellons. Witla Court was the home of the Heywoods, a prosperous Cardiff shipping family. About 15 years ago the estate was developed for private housing and the house has become a pub of the same name

129 Cardiff Post Office drum and fife band at the back of the Post Office in Park Street, 1928

Transport

130/131 Visit of the GWR experimental engine No.5005 'Manorbier Castle' at the General Station heading a London express in 1935. There was much excitement among schoolboys but the experiment was not conspicuously successful. Castle class engines were the biggest and most powerful locomotives on South Wales trains in those days

132 Saint class engine No.2949 'Stanford Court' (built in May 1912 and withdrawn in January 1952) waiting in the General Station to take a stopping train via Marshfield, Newport, Llanwern, Undy, Magor, Severn Tunnel etc. to Bristol in 1935. Temperance Town is in the background

133 Construction of road bridge linking Lower and Upper Waterloo Road, Roath, *c.* 1936. Prior to this a footpath across the bridge in the background and through allotments was the only connection

134 Workmen employed by the Taff Vale Railway *c.*1900, probably in the vicinity of the north end of the West-East Docks with the Rhymney Railway line behind them

135 Women 'emergency conductors' employed by Cardiff Corporation Tramways in the First World War. Although helping the war effort there was much criticism of the innovation

136 Official opening of the single-deck electric tram route to Splott, Roath Dock (Portmanmoor Road) via Bute Terrace and Adam Street on 20 May 1903. The Mayor was Alderman Edward Thomas who was usually known by his Bardic name 'Cochfarf' (Redbeard)—it is the latter which is endorsed on this photograph. The service was started with six trams and was extended to Clive Street terminus when more cars were delivered

137/138 Hall Lewis & Co, were perhaps best known as railway wagon builders and repairers. In their hey-day they were building 50 12-ton coal wagons and repairing 60 every week at their Crown Works, Maindy. Here they are displaying their commercial and public service vehicle coach bodies at Cowbridge Show in the late 1920s. (*Below*) Hall Lewis works' outing to Gloucester and Cheltenham, 1921

139 In 1902 the brothers George (in sidecar) and John Worrell left their home in Norfolk to settle in Cardiff. Using their engineering skill with the priceless added ingredient of hard work each built up businesses which at different times took in cycle dealing and building, 'bus and taxi operating, and garages

140 George Worrell's second cycle shop in 66 Cowbridge Road East. He moved there in 1913 because of the workshop accommodation at the rear which enabled him to service his taxi fleet

141 George Worrell's first cycle shop in 319 Cowbridge Road East, Canton, opened in 1904

142 Worrell's Ely Garage (it was almost opposite St David's Church in Cowbridge Road West) in 1927. Built by George Worrell in 1922 it was taken over by Esso in 1957. At one time in the 1920s it was the only garage in South Wales selling the controversial ROP (Russian) petrol at cut-price for which the proprietor was vilified by the trade and the media

143 This Napier taxi, operated by George Worrell, was hired for a Royal visit to Cardiff in 1912

144 A chauffeur-driven Daimler on the St Fagans road in 1907

145 A 1934 wedding in Roath and a Clyno taxi waits for the bride and groom outside St Margaret's Church

146/147 Types of delivery van used by Harold Leigh Ltd, Penarth Road, in the 30s and 40s. (*Above*) This 4-tonner was supplied new in 1933 by Thornycroft from their East Canal Wharf depot; (*below*) Dennis 5-tonners, supplied new in March 1945 by D. J. Davies, the Merthyr Tydfil coachbuilders

148 A *Western Mail* cartoon by Leslie Illingworth showing Cardiff City director Walter Empsall (with cigar) in conversation with a somewhat down-at-heel supporter in the Bluebirds dressing room. Other easily recognised personalities from the 1920s are George Latham (back view), Jack Kneeshaw and Jack Evans

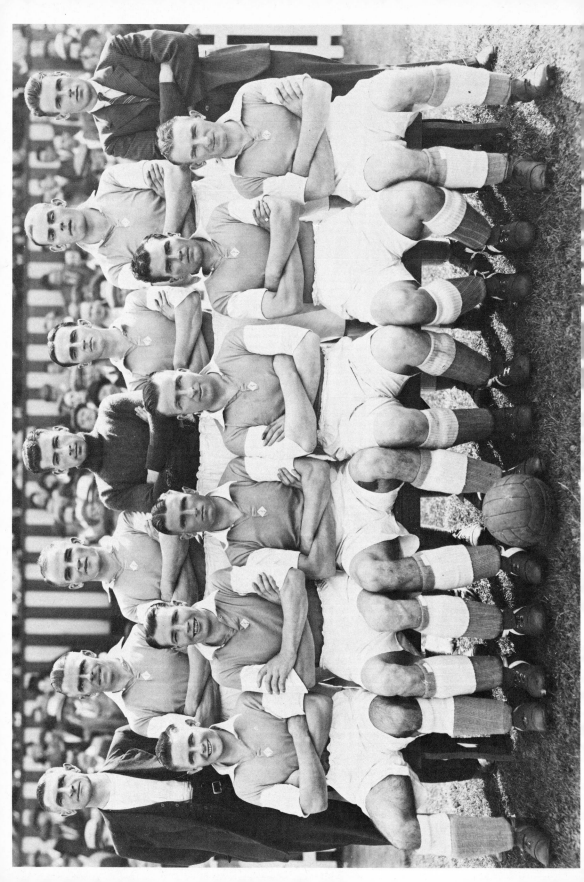

149 (*opposite*) Cardiff City 1936-37. (*Back row, left to right*) Kneeshaw (trainer), Nicholson, Granville, Fielding, Scott, Bassett, H. Smith; (*front row*) Pugh, Talbot, Godfrey (capt.), C. Smith, Pinxton, Ovenstone. This team finished the season eighteenth in the Third Division (South)

150/151 Memories of Cardiff City's promotion season, 1946-47. (*Right*) About to fly from RAF St Athan to Brunswick in Germany to play a BAOR side (they drew 1-1). Fans will recognise Bryn Allen, Fred Stansfield, Alf Sherwood, Ken Hollyman, Billy Rees, and Roy Clarke; (*below*) Fred Stansfield and Billy Rees tog up in the locker room at Ninian Park

152 Cliff Jones 'a dazzling stand-off half' distinguished himself on the rugby field with Cambridge University, Cardiff and Wales before the Second World War and later as an outstanding administrator
From a cigarette card issued with Wills' Embassy *cigarettes*

153 Jack Peterson at the weigh-in with Walter Neusel (Germany) for the second of their two epic 1935 battles at Wembley. On both occasions Peterson was forced to retire because of a badly cut eye
From a cigarette card issued by J. A. Pattreiouex with Senior Service

154 Squaring-up for a bare knuckle fight in the stable yard at the back of the *Cow & Snuffers*, Llandaff North, seventy years ago are (*left*) George Asplin, the landlord, and Enoch 'Knocker' White. Timekeeper was Dick Long, manager of the 'bus depot in nearby Andrew Road. 'This is how they did it in the old days' says W. White, the donor

155 Jim Sullivan who between 1921 and 1946 scored 2,959 goals, 96 tries to make a total of 6,206 points in Rugby League football with Wigan. In northern circles Splott-born Jim is regarded as the greatest rugby player of all time
From a cigarette card issued by J. A. Pattreiouex with Senior Service

156 Cardiff NFS firewomen's gymnastic display team, 1942-43

157 *Blue Pencil*, a very successful hurdler owned by Captain Pat Brain and stabled at Cwrt-yr-ala House, seen at Ely Racecourse in 1933

158 Glamorgan CCC, 1936 (*Back row, left to right*) H. Davies, G. Lavis, C. Smart, G. Reed, A. Dyson, R. Duckfield, T. Brierley; (*front row*) J. Mercer, V. Jenkins, M. Turnbull (captain), D. Davies, E. Davies
From a cigarette card issued with Kings *Cigarettes*

159 Canton Municipal Secondary School, Boswell House senior cricket team, 1928

160 Roath Park School soccer team, 1928-29

161 Moorland supporters will recognise Billy James, Len Dutton and the Stitfall brothers in this
group. They later distinguished themselves in professional football

MOORLAND RD. BOYS (SCHOOL) CHAMPIONS 1935.

162 Cardiff Schools' Football League side pose with their Midland opponents at Villa Park, Birmingham, during the 1945-46 season

163 Cardiff Schools' Football League 54th Season 1949-50. Included in the team was Colin Baker (*second right, seated*) who played for Cardiff City and was capped seven times for Wales

164　Fairwater Juniors FC, 1952-53. The captain was Lance Hayward, former Secretary of
Cardiff City FC

165　Cardiff Schoolboys' under-11 team, joint winners (with Newport) of the Tom Yeoman
Shield

166 Jock Neil will be a familiar face to many who played in the local soccer leagues. He became a referee after a professional career which began with Kilmarnock. After the Second World War he joined Cardiff City but an ankle injury put paid to his playing career

167 A proud moment for 13-year-old John Lloyd (*right*) as he gets close enough to admire the skill of soccer star Duncan Edwards. The Welsh schoolboys had joined the England team at their Porthcawl training camp in November 1957. Three months later Edwards was tragically killed in the Munich air disaster. John Lloyd now lives at Dinas Powis

168   St Francis FC, Splott, season 1926-27

169   Ninian Villa FC with some of their trophies, season 1929-30

170 Clare Gardens FC, September 1930, taken at Llandaff Fields. Goalkeeper was Cliff Kirk who later joined Liverpool as reserve to Elisha Scott and afterwards played for Exeter City

171 Pengam United, winners of Division 4, Cardiff & District League, 1946-47. Their goal average was 66 for, 6 against

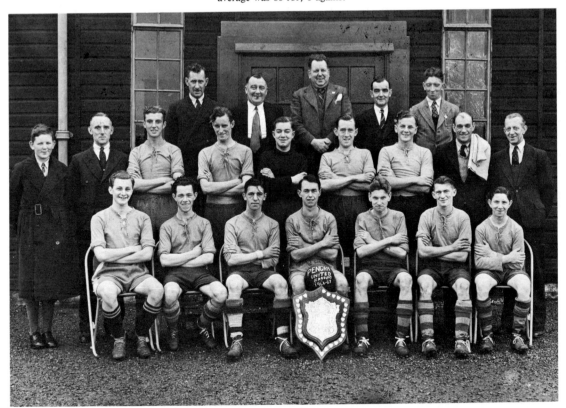

172   Pentyrch Street Baptist FC, 1936 winners of the William Saunders Challenge Cup and
runners-up in the Sunday School League

173   Docks United FC, 1947-48, League Champions and Lennard Cup Winners. Captain was
J. Ugarte. The donor, Tommy Letton, is on the extreme right, back row

174 Avenue Villa FC, Ely, one of the best and most successful post-Second World War teams playing in local amateur football pictured with their cups at the end of the 1950–51 season

175 Thirty-six eager competitors line up in Queen Street at 6.15 am on Saturday 27 June 1903 at the start of the Accountants' Road Walking Race to Caerphilly and back via Draethen, a distance of 22 miles. It was a very warm day and several cases of sunstroke were reported. The winner was G. W. Evans who completed the course in 3 hours 54 minutes 38 seconds

176/177/178/179 Four prominent members of the famous sporting family Pudge of Whitchurch. (*Left to right*) George Pudge, who was Junior Championship runner-up in 1932 and went on to box as a top amateur and was twice All-India Champion in the Second World War; Terry Pudge, Welsh and British Schoolboy Champion in the 1930s, represented the RAF in the 1940s as a feather-weight boxing top class men like Jimmy Ingle, Paddy Dowdall (both European Champions) and Les Merchant, Welsh featherweight Champion; Joe Douglas, whose professional record includes fights against Welsh flyweight champions Jack Kiley, Rufus Enoch and Ron Bishop, and who boxed Jack Pottinger and many others as an amateur under his own name Joe Pudge; Les Gibbon (a nephew) who was Welsh Schoolboy Champion in 1945, Junior Champion 1948-49, and boxed Howard Winstone during his amateur days in 1958

180/181 Mac Williams, the Cardiff-born boxing manager, trainer, and international agent, began his career in the fight game as a heavyweight with the Roath Vale Club. He retired after 18 contests and turned to professional managing. Over the years Mac has managed scores of talented performers and has travelled all over the world. For 15 years, until his death in 1978, Billy Mannings, the man who taught Dai Dower to box, was trainer for the Mac Williams stable. Here Mac is seen (*above*) with heavyweight champion Dick Richardson (*left*) at a social evening; and (*below*) with featherweight champion Howard Winstone and some of his string including Billy Thomas and Terry Gale

182/183 Neighbours and rivals on the banks of the River Taff at Llandaff for many years, the Taff and Cardiff Rowing Clubs were separate organisations until after the Second World War when they amalgamated to become the Llandaff Rowing Club. (*Above*) Taff Rowing Club, 1932. Until the amalgamation they were the oldest club in Wales; (*below*) Llandaff Rowing Club, 1948

184/185 The Cardiff Empire in Queen Street was opened as Levino's Hall in 1887 and renamed the Empire Palace of Varieties when the Stoll Theatre Group took the building over in 1889. It was rebuilt in 1896 and destroyed by fire three years later. In 1900 it was reopened yet again, this time offering the best of music hall in plushy comfort and opulent surroundings, an idea of which can be gained from these photographs which hung for many years on the walls of the *Victoria* on the opposite side of Queen Street. A further reconstruction took place in 1915 and in 1933 it was converted to a cinema. It was renamed the Gaumont in 1954 and finally closed its doors in 1961. All the 'greats' visited the Empire in its hey-day including Vesta Tilley, Eugene Stratton, Chirgwin, Marie Lloyd, Dan Leno, George Robey, Houdini, Little Tich, George Formby Snr, Leslie Henson, Jack Buchanan and Fred Astaire with his sister Adele

186 This is how the Empire looked from Queen Street, *c.*1910

187/188/189 The Empire, during its life as a cinema, featured three resident organists. Many readers will remember them, immaculately attired in white tie and tails, playing their signature tunes at the Compton organ as the illuminated console rose out of the orchestra pit during the interval. The first was Wyndham Lewis (*left*) who stayed for a year until 1934. He had been an assistant to Reginald Foort. Lewis was replaced by Stephen Thomas (*top right*) who remained until 1936. Then came probably the best remembered of the three, Idris Thomas (*bottom right*). 'Idris at the Organ' became a firm favourite and apart from the war years when he served in the RAF remained on the Empire staff until 1947 when cuts in the cinema industry brought this enjoyable musical entertainment to a close. The organ was removed in 1955 and sold to a Bristol church

Very sincerely
Idris
Cardiff

190 Since turning professional in 1949 Stan Stennett has performed equally successfully as stand-up comic, musical entertainer and character actor. He was playing local gigs throughout the 1940s and made the big-time via BBCs 'Welsh Rarebit'. Stan's face is frequently seen on TV where he has appeared on numerous shows ranging from the 'Black and White Minstrels' to 'Crossroads'. Now settled in Rhiwbina, he was educated and brought up in Cardiff living at various times in Ely, Cathays and Whitchurch

191 In 1903 a permanent bandstand was built on the green to the south of the promenade at Roath Park. Previously bands played on the promenade, but a report to the Parks Committee in July 1902 refers to floating bandstands as dangerous which could explain the large crowd waiting, perhaps to be treated to some water music?

192 Accordion bands were extremely popular in the 1930s and Joe Gregory's was one of the best. This band won first prize in the National Accordion Championship Contest at Central Hall, Westminster, London, in 1935

193 The Regal was a popular rendezvous for young dancers in the 30s and 40s. It was swept away when the Gabalfa fly-over was constructed in the early 50s. Western Avenue was opened in July 1933 and the Library in 1928

Memorable Events

194 The Prince of Wales (later King George V) entering Cardiff Castle after laying the foundation stone of the new University College on 28 June 1905

195 Soldiers of the Manchester Regiment guarding Cardiff Docks in the First World War

196 Female munition workers doing their bit for the war effort in the First World War

197 Contingent of the 7th (Cyclists) Battalion of the Welsh Regiment in Newport Road, passing the corner of West Grove, in 1913

198 St Mary's Well Bay, Lavernock, was a big holiday attraction for youngsters in the 1930s. This group of Kent Street, Grangetown boys includes Harry Parsons (*second left, front*) who played for Cardiff City

199 The traditional Whitsun Treat was something to relish, especially when the sun shone, and these children from Heath Gospel Hall, Whitchurch Road, were lucky in 1947

200 The lady on horseback made heads turn as she posed outside Wills's photographic studio, 28 Broadway, in the summer of 1900

201 The little boy on the right of this charming group is Maurice Edelman, later to become well-known as a novelist and politician. His father ran the Cathedral Art Studios in Cowbridge Road, Canton (see No.40 in Book 5)

202 Coach outing from *Great Eastern*, Metal Street, *c.*1935

203 An outing from the *White Swan*, Shakespeare Street, *c.*1946. Kitty Dean, the landlord's daughter, is in the front row. After the death of her father she kept the pub for many years

204 Customers of the *Bird in Hand*, Grangetown, on an outing in the 1920s. The two fiddlers were 'on loan' from Garforth Mortimer's Park Hall orchestra

205 Kent Street Dixielanders celebrate 'VJ Day', August 1945. This happy-go-lucky band of buskers played for dancing in the streets and also assisted in numerous charities

206 Alderman James Griffiths makes a presentation to 11-year-old Leonard Reece of Harrowby Street in recognition of his bravery in rescuing 8-year-old Maureen Divine who fell into the sea lock while playing on the canal bank on 12 February 1944. In the group (*second left, seated*) is Arthur J. Porter, chaplain of 16th Mount Stuart Boys' Brigade, who donated the photograph

207 Curran's employees on the train to London to see Shirley Bassey in her first West End show at the Adelphi Theatre in 1954

208 Staff of Powell Duffryn Associated Collieries Ltd, Cardiff office, on a day's outing to Cheddar in 1939

209 Some of the revellers at the Channel Dry Dock annual Christmas Dance held at the City Hall in 1946

210 Staff of A. McLay & Co. Ltd, the Fairwater printers, about to depart on an outing to Hereford and Symonds Yat in 1936

211 Guest, Keen & Baldwin's employees on an outing from East Moors Works in 1948

212 The Earl of Plymouth (*left*) and Sir Goscombe John (*right*) stand beside the Lord Mayor (Alderman G.Fred Evans) in the Council Chamber at City Hall on 26 October 1936 during the civic ceremony to bestow upon them the Freedom of the City of Cardiff

213 During his year of office the Lord Mayor (Alderman G.Fred Evans) visited every school in the city. Here he is at South Church Street Mixed School on 6 March 1936

214 The Lord Mayor of Cardiff (Alderman G.Fred Evans) performs the corner stone laying ceremony at Roath Library Extension on 20 October 1936. Next to him is George H.Whitaker, the City Engineer